ALEXANDER COLE

Salem Travel Guide 2024-2025

All you need to know about Salem, Budget Planning, Local Cuisine, The witch trials, Haunted sites and beyond!

Contents

1

Chapter 1

About My Trip To Salem

During the fall, I embarked on a journey to Salem, Massachusetts, eager to immerse myself in its rich history and captivating atmosphere. As I strolled through the streets, a mixture of anticipation and apprehension filled me, igniting a sense of curiosity about what awaited me in this historic city.

My first stop was the Salem Witch Trials Memorial, where I was immediately struck by the solemnity of the place. Rows of benches, each inscribed with the names of those accused during the trials, served as a poignant reminder of the human cost of fear and hysteria. Standing amidst the memorial, I couldn't help but feel a deep sense of sadness for the lives lost and the injustices endured.

Venturing into downtown Salem, I discovered a vibrant community bustling with activity. Quaint cafes and shops lined the cobblestone streets, while locals and tourists alike mingled in the lively atmosphere. Despite the weight of history, there was a warmth and friendliness to the city that put me at ease.

One of the highlights of my trip was visiting the Salem Witch Museum, where I delved into the chilling tale of the witch trials through immersive exhibits and informative presentations. The museum offered valuable insights into the events that unfolded in Salem centuries ago, highlighting the resilience of those who stood accused and the enduring legacy of the trials on the city's identity.

As night fell, I joined a ghost tour, eager to experience Salem's supernatural side. Led by lantern light, we wandered through dimly lit streets and alleyways, listening to tales of hauntings and apparitions. While the stories sent shivers down my spine, I found comfort in the camaraderie of my fellow travelers, united by a shared sense of curiosity and excitement.

Leaving Salem behind, I reflected on the experiences that had shaped my journey. From somber moments of reflection at the memorial to the thrill of exploring haunted streets by night, each encounter had left a lasting impression on me. As I boarded the train home, I carried with me not only memories of Salem's storied past but also a newfound appreciation for the power of history to captivate and inspire.

Introduction

Salem, a city brimming with history, mystique, and charm, is nestled in the picturesque state of Massachusetts, USA. Renowned for its witch trials of 1692, Salem attracts visitors from across the globe who seek to unravel its enigmatic past and immerse themselves in its rich cultural tapestry. This essay delves into the essence of Salem, offering a comprehensive exploration of its overview, brief history, and vibrant culture and traditions.

Overview

Salem, with its cobblestone streets, historic landmarks, and maritime allure, exudes an irresistible allure. Situated on the north coast of Massachusetts, Salem overlooks the scenic Salem Harbor, offering breathtaking views of the Atlantic Ocean. Boasting a population of approximately 43,000 residents, Salem is a dynamic city that seamlessly blends its colonial heritage with modern-day vibrancy.

The city's economy thrives on tourism, maritime industries, education, and healthcare. Salem's waterfront, once a bustling hub of maritime commerce, now hosts a myriad of attractions, including museums, galleries, shops, and restaurants. From the iconic Salem Witch Museum to the immersive Peabody Essex Museum, Salem offers an array of cultural experiences that cater to diverse interests.

Visitors to Salem can explore its historic neighborhoods, such as the McIntire Historic District, renowned for its Federal-style architecture, or the Derby Street Historic District, home to the Salem Maritime National Historic Site. Additionally, Salem's vibrant arts scene, encompassing theaters, music venues, and galleries, ensures that there is never a dull moment in this captivating city.

Brief History

Salem's history is as captivating as it is complex, shaped by waves of colonization, maritime trade, and socio-cultural up-heavals. Founded in 1626 by Roger Conant, Salem initially served as a fishing and trading outpost for English settlers seeking economic opportunities in the New World. Its strategic location, abundance of natural resources, and proximity to the Salem Harbor facilitated its rapid growth into a prosperous seaport.

The 17th century witnessed Salem's ascent as a major center of trade, with merchants engaging in lucrative ventures such as the East India trade and the Triangle trade. However, Salem's prosperity was marred by the infamous Salem witch trials of 1692, during which hysteria and paranoia gripped the town, leading to the wrongful execution of 20 individuals accused of witchcraft. This dark chapter in Salem's history continues to fascinate scholars and visitors alike, serving as a poignant reminder of the dangers of intolerance and mass hysteria.

In the 18th and 19th centuries, Salem experienced periods of economic decline followed by revitalization, fueled by industries such as shipbuilding, textiles, and leather manufacturing. The city's architectural landscape flourished during this time, resulting in the preservation of numerous historic buildings and landmarks that stand as testaments to Salem's storied past.

The 20th century saw Salem undergo significant transformations, transitioning from an industrial hub to a vibrant cultural destination. Efforts to preserve its historic character led to the establishment of the Salem Maritime National Historic Site and the restoration of landmarks such as the House of the Seven Gables and the Salem Witch House, ensuring that Salem's heritage would be cherished for generations to come.

Culture and Traditions

Salem's cultural identity is a tapestry woven from diverse threads, reflecting its colonial roots, maritime legacy, and vibrant community spirit. The city's cultural calendar is replete with festivals, events, and traditions that celebrate its heritage and foster a sense of belonging among residents and visitors alike.

One of Salem's most enduring cultural traditions is its annual Halloween celebration, which draws thousands of revelers to the city each October. From haunted tours and costume parades to witchcraft-themed attractions and ghostly storytelling sessions, Salem's Halloween festivities offer a bewitching experience for all ages. The city's association with witchcraft, stemming from the infamous trials of 1692, lends an air of mystique to its Halloween celebrations, making it a must-visit destination for fans of the supernatural.

In addition to Halloween, Salem hosts a plethora of cultural events throughout the year, including the Salem Arts Festival, which showcases the works of local artists through exhibitions, performances, and workshops. The Salem Jazz and Soul Festival, held annually on Salem Willows Park, celebrates the city's musical heritage with live performances by acclaimed musicians from across the region.

Salem's cultural institutions, such as the Peabody Essex Museum and the Salem Witch Museum, play a vital role in preserving and promoting its heritage through exhibitions, educational programs, and community outreach initiatives. These institutions serve as custodians of Salem's past, ensuring that future generations will continue to appreciate and learn from its rich cultural legacy.

Salem is a city steeped in history, culture, and tradition, offering a captivating blend of old-world charm and modern-day vibrancy. From its historic landmarks and maritime heritage to its vibrant arts scene and cultural festivals, Salem invites visitors to embark on a journey of discovery and enchantment. Whether exploring its cobblestone streets or delving into its dark past, one thing is certain: Salem will leave an indelible impression on all who have the privilege of experiencing its splendor.

2

Chapter 2

Getting There

E mbarking on a journey to Salem involves navigating through various transportation options and routes to reach this historic city nestled in the heart of Massachusetts. Whether arriving by air, road, or sea, travelers have a plethora of choices to suit their preferences and convenience. This essay provides a comprehensive guide to getting to Salem, covering transportation options, directions from major cities, and essential airport information.

Transportation Options

Travelers heading to Salem have several transportation options at their disposal, each offering its own advantages in terms of cost, convenience, and flexibility. The following are some of the most common modes of transportation to consider:

1. **Car**: For travelers residing within driving distance of Salem or those who prefer the freedom to explore at their own pace, traveling by car is an excellent option. Salem is easily accessible via major highways, including Interstate 95 and Route 1, which connect the city to neighboring towns and cities.

2. **Train**: Amtrak and the Massachusetts Bay Transportation Authority (MBTA) operate train services to Salem from various destinations along the Northeast Corridor, including Boston, New York City, and Washington, D.C. The Salem station is located in downtown Salem, offering convenient access to the city's attractions and amenities.

3. **Bus**: Several bus companies, including Greyhound and Peter Pan Bus Lines, provide bus services to Salem from major cities across the region. The Salem Transportation Center serves as the city's main bus terminal, offering connections to regional and interstate bus routes.

4. **Ferry**: Travelers seeking a scenic and leisurely journey to Salem can opt for ferry services from Boston's Long Wharf or nearby towns such as Marblehead. Salem Ferry operates seasonal ferry services between May and October, providing a convenient alternative to traditional modes of transportation.

5. **Air**: While Salem does not have its own airport, travelers can fly into nearby airports such as Boston Logan International Airport (BOS) or Manchester-Boston Regional Airport (MHT) and continue their journey to Salem via car, train, or bus.

Choosing the right mode of transportation depends on factors such as distance, budget, and personal preferences. Regardless of the option chosen, travelers can expect a seamless journey to Salem with numerous transportation options available.

Directions from Major Cities

For travelers coming from major cities such as Boston, New York City, and Providence, navigating the route to Salem requires careful planning and consideration of the available transportation options. The following are directions from these major cities to Salem:

1.From Boston, MA:

- **By Car**: Take Interstate 93 North to Interstate 95 North. Continue on Interstate 95 North until reaching Salem. Follow signs for downtown Salem or specific destinations within the city.
- **By Train**: Board an MBTA commuter rail train from Boston's North Station to Salem Station. The journey takes approximately 30-40 minutes, depending on the train schedule.
- **By Bus**: Greyhound and other bus companies operate services from Boston's South Station to Salem Transportation Center. 45 to 60 minutes is how long the trip takes, depending on traffic.

2. From New York City, NY:

- **By Car**: Take Interstate 95 North to Massachusetts. Continue on Interstate 95 North until reaching Salem. Follow signs for downtown Salem or specific destinations within the city.
- **By Train**: Board an Amtrak Northeast Regional or Acela Express train from New York City's Penn Station to Boston's South Station. Transfer to an MBTA commuter rail train to Salem Station.
- **By Bus**: Greyhound and other bus companies operate services from New York City's Port Authority Bus Terminal to Boston's South Station. Transfer to a bus bound for Salem Transportation Center.

3. From Providence, RI:

- **By Car**: Take Interstate 95 North to Massachusetts. Continue on Interstate 95 North until reaching Salem. Follow signs for downtown Salem or specific destinations within the city.
- **By Train**: Board an Amtrak Northeast Regional train from Providence's Union Station to Boston's South Station. Transfer to an MBTA commuter rail train to Salem Station.
- **By Bus**: Peter Pan Bus Lines operates services from Providence's Kennedy Plaza Bus Terminal to Salem Transportation Center.

These directions provide travelers with various options for reaching Salem from major cities in the Northeast region. Whether traveling by car, train, or bus, following these routes ensures a smooth and hassle-free journey to this historic city.

Airport Information

While Salem does not have its own airport, travelers can conveniently access the city via several nearby airports, the most prominent of which are Boston Logan International Airport (BOS) and Manchester-Boston Regional Airport (MHT). Below is essential information about these airports:

1. Boston Logan International Airport (BOS):

- Location: East Boston, Massachusetts
- Distance to Salem: Approximately 15 miles (24 kilometers) southwest of Salem

Transportation Options:

- **Car Rentals**: Several car rental agencies operate at the airport, offering a convenient way to travel to Salem.
- **Public Transportation**: The Massachusetts Bay Transportation Authority (MBTA) operates the Silver Line bus service from the airport to South Station, where travelers can transfer to commuter rail trains bound for Salem.
- **Taxi and Ride-Sharing**: Taxis and ride-sharing services are readily available at the airport, providing direct transportation to Salem.

2. Manchester-Boston Regional Airport (MHT):

- Location: Manchester, New Hampshire
- Distance to Salem: Approximately 46 miles (74 kilometers) north of Salem

- Transportation Options:
- Car Rentals: Several car rental agencies operate at the airport, offering a convenient way to travel to Salem.
- Airport Shuttles: Some hotels in Salem may offer shuttle services to and from Manchester-Boston Regional Airport. Check with your accommodations for availability.
- Taxi and Ride-Sharing: Taxis and ride-sharing services are readily available at the airport, providing direct transportation to Salem.

Both Boston Logan International Airport and Manchester-Boston Regional Airport serve as gateways to Salem, offering travelers a range of transportation options to reach their final destination. Whether arriving from domestic or international locations, these airports provide convenient access to Salem and the surrounding areas.

Getting to Salem involves navigating through various transportation options and routes, each offering its own advantages in terms of convenience and accessibility. Whether traveling by car, train, bus, or plane, visitors to Salem can expect a seamless journey to this historic city, where an array of cultural attractions and experiences await their exploration.

3

Chapter 3

Accommodations

C hoosing the right accommodation is a crucial aspect of any travel experience, and in Salem, Massachusetts, visitors are spoiled for choice. From historic hotels and charming bed and breakfasts to cozy rental properties, Salem offers a diverse array of options to suit every traveler's preferences and budget. This essay provides an in-depth exploration of accommodations in Salem, covering hotels and resorts, bed and breakfasts, and rental properties, highlighting their unique features and amenities.

Hotels and Resorts

Salem boasts a selection of hotels and resorts that cater to travelers seeking comfort, convenience, and luxury during their stay. These establishments combine modern amenities with historic charm, providing guests with a memorable experience that reflects the city's rich heritage. Some of the most notable hotels and resorts in Salem include:

- **The Hawthorne Hotel**: Located in the heart of downtown Salem, The Hawthorne Hotel is a historic landmark renowned for its elegant architecture and timeless charm. Originally built in 1925, this boutique hotel offers 93 guest rooms and suites, each exquisitely furnished with period-style décor and modern amenities. Guests can enjoy fine dining at Nathaniel's restaurant, relax in the cozy Tavern on the Green lounge, or explore nearby attractions such as the Salem Witch Museum and Peabody Essex Museum.
- **The Salem Waterfront Hotel & Suites**: Situated on Pickering Wharf overlooking Salem Harbor, The Salem Waterfront Hotel & Suites offers upscale accommodations with stunning waterfront views. The hotel features 86 spacious guest rooms and suites, each tastefully decorated with nautical-inspired furnishings and plush bedding. Guests can take advantage of amenities such as an indoor pool, fitness center, and complimentary shuttle service to downtown Salem's attractions and restaurants.
- **The Hotel Salem**: Housed in a meticulously restored historic building dating back to the 19th century, The Hotel Salem offers boutique accommodations with a modern twist. Located steps away from Salem's shops, restaurants, and

14

museums, this stylish hotel features 44 guest rooms and suites adorned with vibrant artwork and contemporary furnishings. Guests can unwind at The Roof, the hotel's rooftop bar offering panoramic views of the city, or dine at Counter, a casual café serving locally sourced cuisine.

- **The Salem Inn**: Comprising three historic homes dating back to the 19th century, The Salem Inn offers a charming retreat in the heart of Salem's historic district. Each of the inn's 40 guest rooms and suites is uniquely decorated with period antiques and furnishings, providing guests with a cozy and intimate atmosphere. Amenities include complimentary breakfast, afternoon refreshments, and access to the inn's picturesque courtyard garden.

These hotels and resorts in Salem offer travelers a range of accommodations to suit their preferences, whether they seek luxury, convenience, or historic charm. With their central locations, modern amenities, and attentive service, these establishments ensure a memorable and comfortable stay in the heart of this enchanting city.

Bed and Breakfasts

For travelers seeking a more intimate and personalized lodging experience, Salem's bed and breakfasts offer a cozy retreat away from the hustle and bustle of city life. These charming establishments provide guests with warm hospitality, homemade breakfasts, and a home-away-from-home atmosphere. Some of the top bed and breakfasts in Salem include:

- **Amelia Payson House**: Nestled in the McIntire Historic District, the Amelia Payson House is a beautifully restored Federal-style mansion dating back to 1845. This intimate bed and breakfast features four elegantly appointed guest rooms, each with its own unique décor and modern amenities. Guests can enjoy a gourmet breakfast served in the dining room or relax in the cozy parlor with a book from the inn's extensive library.
- **The Stepping Stone Inn**: Located in a historic Victorian-era home just steps away from Salem's attractions, The Stepping Stone Inn offers guests a tranquil escape with modern comforts. The inn features six spacious guest rooms and suites, each tastefully decorated with antique furnishings and luxurious linens. Guests can start their day with a hearty breakfast served in the sunny dining room or unwind on the inn's wraparound porch overlooking the garden.
- **The Coach House Inn**: Situated in a charming carriage house dating back to the 19th century, The Coach House Inn offers guests a cozy retreat in the heart of Salem's historic district. The inn features seven well-appointed guest rooms, each with its own private entrance and modern amenities. Guests can enjoy a continental breakfast served in the comfort of their room or explore nearby attractions such as the Salem Witch Trials Memorial and House of the Seven Gables.

These bed and breakfasts in Salem provide travelers with a warm and welcoming environment, where they can enjoy personalized service, homemade breakfasts, and a tranquil atmosphere. Whether seeking a romantic getaway or a peaceful retreat, these charming establishments offer a memorable lodging experience in the heart of this historic city.

Rental Properties

For travelers seeking a home-away-from-home experience in Salem, rental properties offer the perfect solution. Whether renting a cozy apartment in the heart of downtown or a spacious house near the waterfront, visitors can enjoy the flexibility, privacy, and convenience of having their own space. Salem offers a variety of rental properties to suit different preferences and budgets, including:

- **Vacation Rentals**: Websites such as Airbnb, VRBO, and HomeAway feature a wide selection of vacation rentals in Salem, ranging from studio apartments and condos to waterfront cottages and historic homes. These properties offer guests the flexibility to customize their stay according to their needs, whether they're traveling solo, with family, or in a group.
- **Long-Term Rentals**: For travelers planning an extended stay in Salem, long-term rental properties provide a comfortable and affordable accommodation option. Many landlords and property management companies offer furnished apartments and houses for rent on a monthly or yearly basis, allowing guests to settle in and experience life like a local in Salem.
- **Vacation Homes**: Ideal for families or groups, vacation homes in Salem offer spacious accommodations with multiple bedrooms, living areas, and amenities such as kitchens,

outdoor patios, and private gardens. These properties provide guests with the freedom to relax, entertain, and explore the city at their own pace, creating cherished memories with loved ones.

Renting a property in Salem offers travelers the freedom to experience the city like a local, with the flexibility to come and go as they please and the convenience of having their own space. Whether staying for a weekend getaway or an extended vacation, rental properties provide guests with a comfortable and convenient home base in this historic and enchanting city.

Finding accommodations in Salem is an integral part of the travel experience, and the city offers a diverse array of options to suit every traveler's preferences and budget. From historic hotels and charming bed and breakfasts to cozy rental properties, Salem provides visitors with a range of lodging choices that reflect the city's rich heritage, warm hospitality, and enchanting atmosphere. Whether seeking luxury, convenience, or a home-away-from-home experience, travelers to Salem are sure to find the perfect accommodation to enhance their stay in this captivating city.

4

Chapter 4

Tours and Activities

S alem, Massachusetts, a city steeped in history, folklore, and maritime heritage, offers visitors a plethora of tours and activities to discover its rich tapestry of culture and intrigue. From guided tours led by knowledgeable experts to self-guided explorations and outdoor adventures, Salem has something to captivate every traveler's interest. This essay delves into the diverse array of tours and activities available in Salem, including guided tours, self-guided tours, and outdoor activities, providing insight into the experiences that await visitors in this enchanting city.

Guided Tours

Guided tours offer visitors an immersive and educational experience, allowing them to delve deeper into Salem's history,
legends, and landmarks with the guidance of knowledgeable
experts. Led by experienced tour guides, these tours provide
insights, anecdotes, and behind-the-scenes access to the city's
most iconic attractions. Some of the most popular guided tours
in Salem include:

- **Salem Witch Trials Tours**: Explore the haunting legacy
  of the Salem Witch Trials with guided tours that trace the
  events leading up to the infamous witch hysteria of 1692.
  Led by historians and storytellers, these tours visit sites
  such as the Salem Witch Trials Memorial, the Witch House,
  and Gallows Hill, shedding light on the trials' historical
  context and lasting impact on Salem's culture.
- **Historic Walking Tours**: Embark on a guided walking
  tour of Salem's historic districts, including the McIntire
  Historic District, Chestnut Street Historic District, and
  Derby Street Historic District. Led by local historians and
  preservationists, these tours showcase the city's architectural gems, colonial-era homes, and maritime heritage,
  offering insights into Salem's evolution from a bustling
  seaport to a vibrant cultural destination.
- **Ghost Tours**: Experience the supernatural side of Salem
  with guided ghost tours that explore the city's haunted
  history and eerie legends. Led by paranormal experts and
  ghost hunters, these tours visit reputedly haunted locations
  such as the Joshua Ward House, Howard Street Cemetery,
  and Old Burying Point Cemetery, sharing spine-chilling

stories and ghostly encounters along the way.

· **Culinary Tours**: Indulge your taste buds on a guided culinary tour of Salem, sampling local specialties, artisanal delights, and international cuisines. Led by food experts and chefs, these tours visit restaurants, bakeries, and markets, offering tastings, demonstrations, and insights into Salem's vibrant culinary scene.

Guided tours in Salem offer travelers an enriching and memorable experience, providing them with the opportunity to learn, explore, and engage with the city's history, culture, and legends under the expert guidance of knowledgeable locals.

Self-Guided Tours

For travelers who prefer to explore independently and at their own pace, self-guided tours offer a flexible and customizable way to experience Salem's attractions, landmarks, and hidden gems. With the aid of maps, audio guides, and smartphone apps, visitors can embark on self-guided adventures that cater to their interests and preferences. Some of the top self-guided tours in Salem include:

· **Heritage Trail**: Follow the Salem Heritage Trail, a self-guided walking tour that winds through the city's historic districts, showcasing notable landmarks, architectural treasures, and maritime sites. Pick up a trail map from the Salem Visitor Center or download the mobile app to explore at your leisure, learning about Salem's history and culture along the way.

- **Literary Landmarks Tour**: Discover Salem's literary heritage with a self-guided tour of the city's literary landmarks and literary-themed attractions. Visit sites such as the House of the Seven Gables, Nathaniel Hawthorne's birthplace, and the Phillips Library, immersing yourself in the world of renowned authors and poets who found inspiration in Salem's storied past.
- **Art Walk**: Embark on a self-guided art walk through Salem's vibrant arts district, exploring galleries, studios, and public art installations. Pick up an art walk map from the Salem Arts Association or download the mobile app to discover local artists, exhibitions, and cultural events happening throughout the city.
- **Harbor Cruise**: Take a self-guided harbor cruise along Salem Harbor, admiring scenic views of the waterfront, lighthouses, and historic ships. Rent a kayak, paddleboard, or sailboat from Salem Harbor Kayak or Mahi Cruises and Charters and set off on your own aquatic adventure, exploring Salem's maritime heritage from a unique perspective.

Self-guided tours in Salem offer travelers the freedom to explore at their own pace, focusing on their interests and preferences while discovering the city's diverse attractions and cultural landmarks.

Outdoor Activities

Beyond its historic streets and cultural attractions, Salem offers outdoor enthusiasts a wealth of opportunities to explore the natural beauty and scenic landscapes of the North Shore region.

From hiking trails and nature reserves to sailing excursions and beachside relaxation, Salem's outdoor activities cater to adventurers of all ages and interests. Some of the top outdoor activities in Salem include:

- **Salem Woods**: Lace up your hiking boots and explore the scenic trails of Salem Woods, a sprawling nature reserve spanning over 300 acres of woodlands, wetlands, and meadows. Follow the Witchcraft Heights Trail or the Salem Woods Trail to discover diverse ecosystems, wildlife habitats, and panoramic views of Salem and the surrounding area.
- **Salem Willows Park**: Enjoy a leisurely stroll along the Salem Willows promenade, a picturesque waterfront park featuring shaded walkways, picnic areas, and panoramic views of Salem Harbor. Rent a paddleboat or kayak from Salem Kayak and explore the harbor's tranquil waters, or indulge in classic seaside activities such as mini-golf, carousel rides, and arcade games.
- **Sailing Excursions**: Set sail on a scenic sailing excursion from Salem Harbor, experiencing the thrill of navigating the open waters aboard a historic schooner or modern yacht. Join a guided sailing tour with Mahi Cruises and Charters or Liberty Fleet of Tall Ships and cruise past iconic landmarks such as Derby Wharf, Winter Island, and Misery Island, learning about Salem's maritime history and seafaring traditions.
- **Beach Day**: Soak up the sun and surf at Salem's nearby beaches, including Willows Beach, Dead Horse Beach, and Juniper Point Beach. Pack a picnic, beach umbrella, and sunscreen and spend the day lounging on the sand, swimming in the ocean, or exploring tide pools and coastal trails.

Outdoor activities in Salem offer travelers the opportunity to connect with nature, unwind in scenic surroundings, and create unforgettable memories amidst the city's natural beauty and maritime charm.

Tours and activities in Salem offer travelers a diverse range of experiences, from guided tours that delve into the city's history and culture to self-guided adventures and outdoor activities that showcase its natural beauty and scenic landscapes. Whether exploring Salem's historic streets, embarking on a sailing excursion, or hiking through the woods, visitors to this enchanting city are sure to find endless opportunities for discovery, adventure, and relaxation.

5

Chapter 5

Crafting the Perfect Travel Itinerary in Salem

C reating a travel itinerary is essential for maximizing your time and experiences while exploring a new destination like Salem, Massachusetts. Whether you're planning a whirlwind one-day visit, a leisurely weekend getaway, or an extended stay, having a well-thought-out itinerary ensures that you make the most of your time and discover the highlights of this historic city. This essay provides detailed itineraries for each type of visit, offering recommendations for attractions, dining, and activities to suit various interests and preferences.

One-Day Itinerary

For travelers with limited time to spare, a one-day itinerary provides a condensed yet fulfilling experience of Salem's rich history, culture, and attractions. This itinerary is designed to showcase the city's highlights while allowing for flexibility and leisurely exploration.

Morning:

- Start your day with breakfast at one of Salem's charming cafes or bakeries, such as Gulu-Gulu Café or Coffee Time Bake Shop.
- Visit the Salem Witch Trials Memorial to pay tribute to the victims of the 1692 witch hysteria and gain insight into this dark chapter of Salem's history.
- Explore the Salem Witch Museum, where interactive exhibits and presentations offer a comprehensive overview of the witch trials and their impact on the city.
- Stroll through the historic streets of downtown Salem, admiring the colonial architecture and browsing the shops and boutiques along Essex Street.

Afternoon:

- Enjoy lunch at one of Salem's local eateries, such as Turner's Seafood or Red's Sandwich Shop.
- Visit the Peabody Essex Museum to explore its diverse collection of art and artifacts, including maritime treasures, Asian art, and contemporary works.
- Take a guided walking tour of the McIntire Historic District

or Derby Street Historic District to learn about Salem's architectural heritage and notable landmarks.
- Stop by the House of the Seven Gables, made famous by Nathaniel Hawthorne's novel, and explore the historic mansion and gardens overlooking Salem Harbor.

Evening:

- Dine at one of Salem's waterfront restaurants, such as Sea Level Oyster Bar or Finz Seafood & Grill, and enjoy fresh seafood and scenic views of the harbor.
- Attend a performance or event at one of Salem's theaters or music venues, such as the Salem Theatre Company or the Cabot Performing Arts Center.
- End your day with a leisurely stroll along the Salem Maritime National Historic Site, soaking in the ambiance of the waterfront and admiring the historic ships and maritime exhibits.

This one-day itinerary offers a taste of Salem's diverse attractions and experiences, allowing travelers to immerse themselves in the city's culture and history while making the most of their time.

Weekend Getaway

For travelers seeking a weekend getaway to unwind and explore Salem at a leisurely pace, this itinerary offers a mix of cultural experiences, outdoor activities, and culinary delights.

Day 1:

- Start your weekend with breakfast at a local diner or breakfast spot, such as Ugly Mug Diner or A&J King Bakery.
- Visit the Salem Witch Museum to delve into the history and mythology of the Salem witch trials through exhibits and presentations.
- Explore the historic Salem Witch Trials Memorial and pay your respects to the victims of the witch hysteria.
- Enjoy a scenic harbor cruise or sailing excursion to take in views of Salem's waterfront and historic landmarks from the water.
- Have dinner at a cozy restaurant or tavern, such as Opus or The Lobster Shanty, and savor New England classics like clam chowder and lobster rolls.

Day 2:

- Start your day with a visit to the Peabody Essex Museum to explore its world-class collection of art, culture, and maritime history.
- Take a guided walking tour of Salem's historic districts, such as the McIntire Historic District or Chestnut Street Historic District, to admire the city's colonial architecture and notable landmarks.
- Visit the House of the Seven Gables, where you can tour the historic mansion, gardens, and seaside paths overlooking Salem Harbor.
- Enjoy lunch at a waterfront restaurant or cafe, such as Sea Level Oyster Bar or Salem Waterfront Hotel & Suites.
- Spend the afternoon browsing the shops and boutiques

along Essex Street, picking up souvenirs, gifts, and local artisanal products.
- End your weekend getaway with a leisurely stroll along Salem's scenic waterfront, watching the sunset over the harbor and reflecting on your time in this historic city.

This weekend getaway itinerary offers travelers the opportunity to relax, explore, and immerse themselves in Salem's culture and charm at a leisurely pace.

Extended Stay Options

For travelers planning an extended stay in Salem, whether for work, study, or leisure, this itinerary offers a mix of cultural experiences, outdoor activities, and day trips to nearby attractions.

Week 1:

- Explore Salem's historic districts and landmarks, including the Salem Witch Trials Memorial, the House of the Seven Gables, and the Peabody Essex Museum.
- Attend cultural events and festivals happening throughout the city, such as the Salem Arts Festival or the Salem Haunted Happenings.
- Take a day trip to nearby attractions, such as the historic town of Marblehead, the coastal communities of Gloucester and Rockport, or the picturesque Crane Beach in Ipswich.

Week 2:

- Dive deeper into Salem's history and culture with guided tours and lectures offered by local historians, preservationists, and experts.
- Participate in hands-on workshops and classes at the Salem Arts Association, the Salem Witch Museum, or the Salem Maritime National Historic Site.
- Explore Salem's culinary scene with food tours, cooking classes, and tastings at local restaurants, breweries, and specialty shops.

Week 3:

- Immerse yourself in nature with outdoor activities such as hiking in Salem Woods, kayaking or paddleboarding on Salem Harbor, or birdwatching at Winter Island Park.
- Take a scenic drive along the North Shore Coastal Scenic Byway, stopping at coastal towns, lighthouses, and scenic overlooks along the way.
- Relax and recharge with wellness activities such as yoga classes, spa treatments, or meditation sessions offered at local studios and wellness centers.

This extended stay itinerary allows travelers to fully immerse themselves in Salem's culture, history, and natural beauty while enjoying a diverse range of experiences and activities throughout their stay.

Crafting a travel itinerary for exploring Salem allows visitors to tailor their experiences to their interests, preferences, and time constraints. Whether planning a one-day visit, a weekend getaway, or an extended stay, travelers can discover the highlights of this historic city while immersing themselves in its culture, history, and charm. With a well-thought-out itinerary, visitors to Salem can make the most of their time and create unforgettable memories in this enchanting destination.

6

Chapter 6

Navigating Travel Costs

P lanning a trip to Salem, Massachusetts involves careful consideration of travel costs to ensure that your experience is both enjoyable and affordable. From transportation and accommodation to dining and attractions, understanding the average expenses and implementing budget-saving strategies can help you make the most of your travel budget. This essay provides a detailed exploration of travel costs associated with visiting Salem, offering insights into budget planning, average expenses, and tips for saving money while exploring this historic city.

Budget Planning

Budget planning is the first step in preparing for your trip to Salem, allowing you to establish a realistic spending limit and allocate funds to different aspects of your journey. To create an effective budget plan, consider the following factors:

- **Transportation**: Determine how you will travel to Salem, whether by car, train, bus, or plane, and research the associated costs, including airfare, gas, tolls, parking fees, and public transportation fares.
- **Accommodation**: Research lodging options in Salem, from budget-friendly hotels and hostels to luxury resorts and vacation rentals, and compare prices, amenities, and location to find the best value for your budget.
- **Food and Dining**: Estimate your daily food expenses based on the cost of meals, snacks, and beverages, taking into account dining out at restaurants, purchasing groceries, or cooking your own food if you have access to a kitchen.
- **Activities and Attractions**: Research the cost of admission fees, guided tours, recreational activities, and cultural attractions in Salem, and prioritize your must-see destinations based on your interests and budget.
- **Miscellaneous Expenses**: Factor in additional expenses such as souvenirs, transportation within Salem, travel insurance, and unexpected costs that may arise during your trip.

By establishing a budget plan that accounts for all aspects of your travel expenses, you can ensure that you have sufficient funds to cover your needs and enjoy a stress-free experience in

Salem.

Average Expenses

To help you estimate the average expenses associated with visiting Salem, here is a breakdown of typical costs for transportation, accommodation, dining, and activities:

1. **Transportation**:

- **Airfare**: Depending on your location and travel dates, round-trip flights to nearby airports such as Boston Logan International Airport or Manchester-Boston Regional Airport may range from $100 to $500 or more per person.
- **Gas**: If traveling by car, estimate the cost of gas based on the distance to Salem and current fuel prices, budgeting approximately $50 to $100 or more for round-trip transportation.
- **Public Transportation**: Salem offers affordable public transportation options such as buses and commuter rail services, with fares ranging from $2 to $10 per ride depending on the distance traveled.

2. **Accommodation**:

- **Hotels**: The average cost of a one-night stay at a mid-range hotel in Salem ranges from $100 to $200 or more, depending on the time of year, location, and amenities.
- **Bed and Breakfasts**: Prices for bed and breakfast accommodations in Salem typically range from $100 to $250 per night, with variations based on room size, amenities, and

included meals.

- **Vacation Rentals**: Renting a vacation home or apartment in Salem may cost between $150 and $400 or more per night, depending on the size, location, and amenities of the property.

3. Dining:

- **Meals**: Dining out at restaurants in Salem can range from $10 to $50 or more per person for breakfast, lunch, or dinner, depending on the type of cuisine, restaurant atmosphere, and menu selections.
- **Groceries**: Purchasing groceries and preparing your own meals can help save money on dining expenses, with average costs for groceries ranging from $50 to $100 or more per person per week, depending on dietary preferences and meal planning.

4. Activities and Attractions:

- Admission Fees: The cost of admission to museums, historic sites, and attractions in Salem varies, with average prices ranging from $10 to $30 or more per person, depending on the venue and included amenities.
- Guided Tours: Guided walking tours, ghost tours, and specialty tours in Salem may range from $15 to $50 or more per person, depending on the duration, content, and expertise of the tour guide.

These average expenses provide a general overview of the costs associated with visiting Salem and can help you budget and plan accordingly for your trip.

Tips for Saving Money

To make the most of your travel budget and save money while exploring Salem, consider implementing the following tips and strategies:

- **Travel Off-Season**: Visiting Salem during the shoulder seasons of spring and fall can help you save money on transportation, accommodation, and attractions, as prices tend to be lower and crowds are smaller compared to peak tourist seasons.
- **Book in Advance**: Take advantage of early booking discounts and promotional offers when reserving flights, hotels, rental cars, and activities in Salem, as prices may increase closer to your travel dates.
- **Opt for Budget-Friendly Accommodations**: Consider staying at budget-friendly accommodations such as hostels, motels, or vacation rentals, which offer affordable rates and often include amenities such as kitchenettes or complimentary breakfast.
- **Dine Strategically**: Save money on dining expenses by eating at local cafes, bakeries, and food trucks, where prices are often lower compared to sit-down restaurants. Take advantage of happy hour specials, early bird discounts, and prix-fixe menus for dining out on a budget.
- **Utilize Public Transportation**: Take advantage of Salem's affordable public transportation options, such as buses and commuter rail services, to get around the city and explore

nearby attractions without the need for a rental car.
- **Seek Out Free or Low-Cost Activities**: Take advantage of free or low-cost activities and attractions in Salem, such as walking tours, hiking trails, public parks, and cultural events, should have a cultural and historical experience of the city without going broke.
- **Pack Light and Bring Essentials**: Avoid excess baggage fees and save money on travel essentials by packing light and bringing only what you need for your trip to Salem. Consider bringing reusable water bottles, snacks, and travel-sized toiletries to minimize expenses during your stay.

By implementing these tips and strategies, you can stretch your travel budget and enjoy a memorable and affordable experience in Salem without sacrificing quality or comfort.

Navigating travel costs while planning a trip to Salem involves careful budget planning, understanding average expenses, and implementing strategies for saving money without compromising on the quality of your experience. By establishing a realistic budget plan, researching average costs, and utilizing budget-saving tips, travelers can make the most of their travel budget and enjoy a memorable and affordable trip to this historic city.

7

Chapter 7

Ensuring Safety and Well-Being

Safety is a paramount concern for travelers exploring new destinations, and Salem, Massachusetts, is no exception. While this historic city offers a wealth of cultural attractions and scenic landmarks to discover, it's essential to prioritize safety and well-being throughout your visit. This essay provides a detailed exploration of staying safe in Salem, including general safety tips, emergency contacts, and health precautions to help travelers enjoy a worry-free experience in this enchanting destination.

General Safety Tips

- **Stay Aware of Your Surroundings**: Remain vigilant and aware of your surroundings while exploring Salem, especially in crowded areas, tourist attractions, and nightlife districts. Keep valuables secure and avoid displaying expensive jewelry, electronics, or large sums of cash.
- **Use Caution at Night**: Exercise caution when venturing out at night, especially in unfamiliar areas or dimly lit streets. Stick to well-lit and populated areas, and avoid walking alone after dark. Consider using transportation services such as taxis or rideshare apps for added safety.
- **Follow Traffic Laws**: Whether driving, biking, or walking in Salem, obey traffic laws, signals, and signage to ensure your safety and the safety of others. Use designated crosswalks when crossing the street, and be mindful of vehicles, cyclists, and pedestrians sharing the road.
- **Stay Hydrated and Sun Protected**: Salem experiences varying weather conditions throughout the year, including hot summers and cold winters. Stay hydrated, wear sunscreen, and dress appropriately for the weather to prevent sunburn, heat exhaustion, or hypothermia depending on the season.
- **Practice Water Safety**: If enjoying recreational activities on or near the water, such as swimming, boating, or kayaking, prioritize water safety by wearing life jackets, swimming in designated areas, and observing posted warning signs and advisories.
- **Respect Local Laws and Customs**: Familiarize yourself with local laws, regulations, and customs in Salem, including alcohol consumption, smoking restrictions, and cultural sensitivities. Show respect for the city's residents, land-

marks, and traditions to avoid unnecessary conflicts or misunderstandings.

- **Trust Your Instincts**: Trust your instincts and intuition when assessing potential risks or unfamiliar situations in Salem. If something feels unsafe or uncomfortable, remove yourself from the situation and seek assistance from local authorities or trusted individuals.

Emergency Contacts

Knowing where to turn for assistance and support in Salem during an emergency or crisis is crucial. Familiarize yourself with the following emergency contacts and resources:

- **911**: Dial 911 for emergencies requiring immediate assistance from police, fire, or medical services in Salem. Provide clear and concise information about the nature of the emergency, your location, and any relevant details to ensure a prompt response from emergency responders.
- **Salem Police Department**: Contact the Salem Police Department non-emergency line at (978) 744-1212 for non-life-threatening situations, reporting incidents, or seeking assistance from law enforcement officers in Salem. Be prepared to provide details about the incident or concern and follow instructions from the dispatcher.
- **Salem Fire Department**: For fire-related emergencies, including fires, explosions, or hazardous materials incidents, contact the Salem Fire Department at (978) 744-0171. Evacuate the area immediately, alert others to the danger, and await instructions from firefighters upon their arrival.
- **Emergency Medical Services (EMS)**: In the event of a medi-

cal emergency or injury requiring urgent medical attention, dial 911 to request assistance from EMS personnel. Provide information about the nature of the medical issue, the patient's condition, and the location for efficient response and treatment.

- **Poison Control Center**: If you or someone else experiences poisoning or exposure to toxic substances in Salem, contact the Poison Control Center at 1-800-222-1222 for immediate assistance and guidance. Provide information about the type of poison or substance involved and follow instructions from the poison control specialist.
- **Consular Services**: For international travelers requiring assistance with passport issues, legal matters, or emergency situations abroad, contact your country's consulate or embassy in the United States for consular services and support.
- **Local Hospitals and Medical Facilities**: Familiarize yourself with the locations and contact information for local hospitals and medical facilities in Salem, including emergency rooms, urgent care centers, and pharmacies, in case of medical emergencies or health concerns during your visit.

Health Precautions

- **COVID-19 Safety Measures**: Stay informed about current COVID-19 guidelines and restrictions in Salem, including mask mandates, social distancing requirements, and vaccination recommendations. Follow recommended safety protocols, such as wearing masks in indoor public spaces, practicing hand hygiene, and avoiding large gatherings to reduce the risk of COVID-19 transmission.
- **Stay Hygienic**: Practice good hygiene habits, such as wash-

ing your hands frequently with soap and water for at least 20 seconds, using hand sanitizer with at least 60% alcohol when handwashing facilities are unavailable, and avoiding touching your face, mouth, and eyes with unwashed hands.

- **Stay Vaccinated**: Stay up-to-date on routine vaccinations and immunizations recommended by healthcare professionals before traveling to Salem. Consider getting vaccinated against preventable diseases such as influenza, measles, and COVID-19 to protect yourself and others during your visit.

- **Stay Informed about Health Risks**: Stay informed about potential health risks and hazards in Salem, including environmental factors, seasonal illnesses, and local outbreaks. Monitor local health advisories and updates from reputable sources such as the Centers for Disease Control and Prevention (CDC) and the Massachusetts Department of Public Health (DPH).

- **Seek Medical Care if Needed**: If you experience symptoms of illness or injury during your visit to Salem, seek medical care promptly from a healthcare provider or medical facility. Describe your symptoms, travel history, and any relevant information to assist healthcare professionals in providing appropriate care and treatment.

By following these general safety tips, accessing emergency contacts when needed, and prioritizing health precautions, travelers can enjoy a safe and worry-free experience in Salem, Massachusetts. Whether exploring historic landmarks, enjoying outdoor activities, or sampling local cuisine, taking proactive measures to ensure safety and well-being enhances the overall travel experience and fosters a sense of confidence and security throughout your visit.

8

Chapter 8

Finding the Perfect Time to Experience Salem

C hoosing the best time to visit Salem, Massachusetts involves consideration of weather conditions, tourist seasons, and special events that enhance the city's cultural offerings and historical charm. Whether you're drawn to Salem's vibrant autumn foliage, summer festivities, or off-peak tranquility, this guide provides insights into timing your visit for an unforgettable experience in this enchanting destination.

Weather Conditions

Salem experiences four distinct seasons, each offering its own unique climate and ambiance:

1. Spring (March to May): Spring in Salem brings mild tem-

peratures and blooming flowers, making it an ideal time for outdoor exploration and cultural activities. Average temperatures range from 40°F to 60°F (4°C to 15°C), with occasional rain showers and cool evenings.

2. Summer (June to August): Summer is the peak tourist season in Salem, characterized by warm temperatures, sunny skies, and bustling streets. Average temperatures range from 60°F to 80°F (15°C to 27°C), with occasional heatwaves and humidity. Summer is perfect for outdoor festivals, beach days, and sightseeing.

3. Fall (September to November): Fall is arguably the most popular time to visit Salem, known for its stunning foliage, crisp air, and Halloween festivities. Average temperatures range from 50°F to 70°F (10°C to 21°C), with peak foliage occurring in October. Fall foliage tours, haunted attractions, and harvest festivals abound during this season.

4. Winter (December to February): Winter brings cold temperatures and occasional snowfall to Salem, creating a picturesque winter wonderland. Average temperatures range from 20°F to 40°F (-6°C to 4°C), with shorter days and longer nights. Winter is ideal for cozying up by the fireplace, exploring indoor attractions, and enjoying seasonal events.

Peak Tourist Seasons

Salem experiences peak tourist seasons during the summer and fall months, when visitors flock to the city to experience its historical sites, cultural events, and seasonal attractions. Understanding peak tourist seasons can help you plan your visit and navigate crowds more effectively:

1. Summer (June to August): Summer is the busiest time of year in Salem, with peak tourist activity occurring from late June through August. During this time, streets, restaurants, and attractions may be crowded, and accommodations may book up quickly. Advance reservations are recommended for lodging, dining, and activities.

2. Fall (September to November): Fall is another peak tourist season in Salem, particularly during October, when the city hosts its renowned Haunted Happenings festival. Visitors come from near and far to experience Halloween-themed events, ghost tours, and historical reenactments. Plan ahead for accommodations and activities, especially during weekends and around Halloween.

Special Events and Festivals

Salem hosts a variety of special events and festivals throughout the year, offering visitors unique opportunities to immerse themselves in the city's culture, history, and traditions. Some notable events include:

1. Salem Arts Festival (June): Celebrating the vibrant arts community of Salem, the Salem Arts Festival features live music, art installations, performances, and interactive activities throughout downtown Salem. Visitors can explore galleries, studios, and outdoor exhibits showcasing the work of local artists.

2. Salem Heritage Days (August): Salem Heritage Days is a week-long celebration of the city's rich history and maritime heritage, featuring historical reenactments, walking tours, harbor cruises, and family-friendly activities. High-

lights include the Salem Maritime Festival, Essex Street Fair, and fireworks over Salem Harbor.

3. Haunted Happenings (October): Haunted Happenings is Salem's signature Halloween festival, attracting thousands of visitors each year with its array of spooky events and attractions. From ghost tours and haunted houses to costume balls and parades, there's something for everyone to enjoy during this month-long celebration of all things eerie and supernatural.

4. Salem Film Fest (March): The Salem Film Fest showcases documentary films from around the world, offering audiences thought-provoking perspectives on diverse topics and issues. Film screenings, panel discussions, and filmmaker Q&A sessions take place at venues throughout Salem, providing opportunities for cultural enrichment and dialogue.

By planning your visit to coincide with special events and festivals in Salem, you can enhance your experience and immerse yourself in the city's vibrant culture and community spirit.

Choosing the Best Time to Visit

When determining the best time to visit Salem, consider your personal preferences, interests, and priorities. Whether you're drawn to the lively atmosphere of summer, the colorful foliage of fall, or the quiet charm of winter, there's something to enjoy in Salem year-round. Take into consideration the following advice to maximize your visit:

1. Peak Season vs. Off-Peak: If you prefer fewer crowds and lower prices, consider visiting Salem during the off-peak seasons of spring or winter. You'll have more flexibility in accommodations, dining options, and activities, allowing for a more relaxed and authentic experience.

2. Seasonal Activities: Tailor your visit to Salem based on seasonal activities and attractions. Whether it's attending the Salem Arts Festival in summer, exploring fall foliage in autumn, or enjoying holiday festivities in winter, aligning your visit with seasonal highlights ensures a memorable and enriching experience.

3. Budget and Availability: Consider your budget and availability when planning your visit to Salem. Prices for accommodations, transportation, and activities may vary depending on the time of year, so research rates and availability in advance to secure the best deals.

4. Personal Preferences: Ultimately, the best time to visit Salem is whenever it aligns with your personal preferences, interests, and schedule. Whether you're seeking outdoor adventures, cultural experiences, or historical insights, Salem offers something for every traveler to enjoy year-round.

Choosing the best time to visit Salem involves consideration of weather conditions, tourist seasons, and special events that enhance the city's cultural offerings and historical charm. Whether you're drawn to the vibrant energy of summer, the colorful foliage of fall, or the cozy atmosphere of winter, planning your visit accordingly ensures a memorable and enriching experience in this enchanting destination. By aligning your visit with your interests, preferences, and priorities, you can make the most of your time in Salem and create lasting memories of your journey to this historic city.

9

Chapter 9

Savoring Salem

S alem, Massachusetts, is not only celebrated for its rich history and cultural heritage but also for its vibrant culinary scene. From fresh seafood and New England classics to international flavors and artisanal delights, Salem offers a diverse array of dining options to satisfy every palate. In this comprehensive guide, we'll delve into the local cuisine, highlight top restaurants and cafes, and explore popular dishes that are must-try when visiting this historic city.

Local Cuisine

Salem's culinary landscape is deeply rooted in New England's rich culinary traditions, featuring fresh seafood, hearty comfort food, and locally sourced ingredients. Some defining characteristics of Salem's local cuisine include:

- **Seafood**: Located along the coast of Massachusetts, Salem boasts access to fresh seafood from the Atlantic Ocean. Lobster, clams, oysters, and fish feature prominently on menus throughout the city, prepared in a variety of delicious ways, from classic clam chowder to seafood boils and lobster rolls.
- **New England Classics**: Salem is known for its interpretation of classic New England dishes, such as clam chowder, fish and chips, and baked beans. These hearty and comforting meals reflect the region's maritime heritage and agricultural roots, often served with a side of freshly baked bread or cornbread.
- **Farm-to-Table Fare**: With a growing emphasis on sustainability and locally sourced ingredients, many restaurants in Salem embrace the farm-to-table movement, showcasing the bounty of the region's farms, orchards, and artisan producers. Farm-fresh vegetables, artisanal cheeses, and pasture-raised meats are featured prominently on menus, highlighting the flavors of the season.
- **International Influences**: Salem's culinary scene also reflects the city's diverse cultural influences, with restaurants offering a wide range of international cuisines, including Italian, Mexican, Mediterranean, and Asian fare. Visitors can explore global flavors while enjoying a meal in one of Salem's charming eateries or cafes.

Restaurants and Cafes

- **Finz Seafood & Grill**: Located on the waterfront, Finz Seafood & Grill is a popular dining destination known for its fresh seafood, innovative cocktails, and scenic views of Salem Harbor. Highlights include the raw bar offerings, lobster mac and cheese, and seafood paella.
- **Ledger Restaurant & Bar**: Housed in a historic bank building, Ledger Restaurant & Bar offers a unique dining experience with its contemporary American cuisine and elegant ambiance. Dishes showcase locally sourced ingredients and creative culinary techniques, with options ranging from wood-fired pizzas to dry-aged steaks.
- **Gulu-Gulu Cafe**: This eclectic cafe and bar in downtown Salem is a favorite among locals and visitors alike, offering a cozy atmosphere, live music, and an extensive selection of craft beers and ciders. The menu features globally inspired dishes, artisanal sandwiches, and decadent desserts.
- **Turner's Seafood**: Established in 1994, Turner's Seafood is a family-owned restaurant specializing in fresh seafood and classic New England fare. Located in the historic Lyceum Hall, Turner's offers a casual yet refined dining experience, with highlights including New England clam chowder, lobster bisque, and seafood platters.
- **A&J King Bakery**: For artisanal pastries, bread, and coffee, look no further than A&J King Bakery. This beloved bakery in downtown Salem is known for its handcrafted croissants, fruit tarts, and specialty cakes, along with a selection of freshly brewed coffee and espresso drinks.
- **Opus**: As one of Salem's premier dining destinations, Opus offers a sophisticated atmosphere and creative cuisine with

global influences. From sushi and sashimi to gourmet burgers and wood-fired pizzas, Opus delivers a diverse dining experience that caters to a range of tastes and preferences.

Popular Dishes to Try

- **Lobster Roll**: A quintessential New England dish, the lobster roll features tender chunks of lobster meat served on a buttered and toasted bun, often accompanied by a side of coleslaw or potato chips. Salem's waterfront restaurants and seafood shacks offer some of the best lobster rolls in the region.
- **Clam Chowder**: Salem's version of clam chowder is a creamy and comforting soup made with tender clams, potatoes, onions, and celery, flavored with bacon and herbs. Enjoy a bowl of clam chowder at a local restaurant or seafood market for a taste of New England's culinary heritage.
- **Fish and Chips**: Crispy battered fish served with French fries and tartar sauce, fish and chips is a classic comfort food dish that can be found at pubs, seafood restaurants, and waterfront eateries throughout Salem. Enjoy this hearty meal with a cold beer or lemonade for a satisfying dining experience.
- **Baked Beans**: Baked beans are a staple of traditional New England cuisine, made with navy beans, molasses, brown sugar, and salt pork, slow-cooked until tender and flavorful. Enjoy baked beans as a side dish or as part of a hearty breakfast spread with eggs, toast, and sausage.
- **Salem Harbor Cocktail**: For a taste of Salem's maritime heritage, try the Salem Harbor Cocktail, a refreshing drink made with rum, cranberry juice, lime juice, and simple

syrup, garnished with a lime wedge or fresh cranberries. Sip on this cocktail while enjoying views of Salem Harbor at a waterfront bar or restaurant.

· **Apple Cider Donuts**: During the fall season, indulge in Salem's famous apple cider donuts, made with fresh apple cider, cinnamon, and nutmeg, then dusted with powdered sugar or cinnamon sugar. These irresistible treats are a favorite at local orchards, farmers' markets, and bakeries throughout the city.

Salem's culinary scene offers a diverse array of flavors, from fresh seafood and New England classics to international cuisine and artisanal delights. Whether you're savoring a lobster roll on the waterfront, indulging in clam chowder at a cozy cafe, or sampling global flavors at a trendy restaurant, Salem's culinary landscape promises to delight and satisfy every palate. By exploring local cuisine, dining at top restaurants and cafes, and sampling popular dishes, visitors can embark on a culinary journey through Salem that celebrates the city's rich history, culture, and culinary traditions.

Chapter 10

Unlocking Salem

As you plan your visit to Salem, Massachusetts, you'll find a wealth of resources available to enhance your experience and ensure a memorable journey. From useful websites and mobile apps to recommended reading and visitor information centers, these additional resources provide valuable insights, practical information, and insider tips to help you make the most of your time in this historic city. In this comprehensive guide, we'll explore the various resources available to travelers and highlight how they can assist in planning and navigating your visit to Salem.

Useful Websites and Apps

1. Destination Salem (Website): Destination Salem is the official tourism website for the city of Salem, offering comprehensive information on attractions, events, dining, accommodations, and transportation options. Visitors can

access maps, itineraries, and travel tips to help plan their trip and make the most of their time in Salem.

2. Salem.org (Website): Salem.org is another valuable resource for travelers, providing detailed guides, articles, and recommendations on things to do, places to eat, and where to stay in Salem. The website features curated lists of attractions, events, and businesses, making it easy to discover hidden gems and local favorites.

3. Salem Insider (Mobile App): The Salem Insider mobile app is a handy tool for travelers, offering insider tips, self-guided tours, and interactive maps to navigate the city. Users can explore themed itineraries, access real-time updates on events and attractions, and discover special offers and discounts from local businesses.

4. Google Maps (Mobile App): Google Maps is indispensable for navigating Salem and its surrounding areas, providing detailed maps, driving directions, and public transportation routes. Users can search for nearby attractions, restaurants, and points of interest, and plan their travel itinerary with ease.

5. TripAdvisor (Website and Mobile App): TripAdvisor is a trusted platform for traveler reviews and recommendations, allowing users to discover top-rated hotels, restaurants, and attractions in Salem. Visitors can read reviews, view photos, and compare prices to make informed decisions when planning their trip.

6. Weather.com (Website and Mobile App): Stay updated on Salem's weather forecast and current conditions with the Weather.com website or mobile app. Access hourly and daily forecasts, radar maps, and severe weather alerts to plan outdoor activities and dress accordingly during your

visit.

Visitor Information Centers

- **Salem Visitor Center**: Located in the heart of downtown Salem, the Salem Visitor Center serves as a central hub for tourist information, offering maps, brochures, and expert advice from knowledgeable staff. Visitors can learn about upcoming events, guided tours, and attractions, and purchase tickets for tours and activities.

- **Salem Maritime National Historic Site**: Operated by the National Park Service, the Salem Maritime National Historic Site provides visitors with insights into Salem's maritime history, including guided tours, exhibits, and ranger-led programs. The visitor center offers educational resources, interactive exhibits, and information on nearby attractions and points of interest.

- **Salem Witch Museum**: The Salem Witch Museum offers a fascinating glimpse into the history of the Salem witch trials through multimedia exhibits, artifacts, and presentations. Visitors can stop by the museum's information desk for assistance with directions, recommendations, and inquiries about witchcraft-related attractions and events in Salem.

- **Salem Witch Trials Memorial**: Located adjacent to the Old Burying Point Cemetery, the Salem Witch Trials Memorial commemorates the victims of the witch trials with a series of memorial benches inscribed with the names of those who were accused and executed. Visitors can reflect on the solemn history of the witch trials and learn about their significance from interpretive panels at the memorial site.

Accessing additional resources such as useful websites and apps, recommended reading, and visitor information centers can greatly enhance your experience when visiting Salem, Massachusetts. Whether you're seeking practical travel advice, historical insights, or cultural recommendations, these resources provide valuable assistance and guidance to help you plan and navigate your journey through this historic city. By leveraging the wealth of information and expertise available, travelers can unlock the secrets of Salem and create lasting memories of their visit to this enchanting destination.

Conclusion

In conclusion, navigating and exploring Salem, Massachusetts, is a journey filled with rich history, diverse culture, and culinary delights. Through this comprehensive guide, we've delved into various aspects of planning and experiencing Salem, from understanding its historical significance to discovering its vibrant culinary scene and accessing additional resources for a well-rounded visit.

Salem's allure lies in its ability to captivate visitors with its intriguing past, embodied by landmarks such as the Salem Witch Trials Memorial and the Salem Maritime National Historic Site.

By immersing oneself in Salem's history and culture, travelers gain a deeper appreciation for the city's legacy and enduring charm.

Salem's culinary landscape offers a tantalizing array of flavors and dishes, from fresh seafood and New England classics to international cuisine and artisanal creations. Exploring local eateries, cafes, and bakeries allows visitors to savor the essence of Salem while indulging in gastronomic delights.

leveraging useful websites, mobile apps, and recommended reading materials provides travelers with valuable insights, practical information, and insider tips to enhance their Salem experience. Whether accessing real-time updates on events, discovering hidden gems, or gaining historical context through literature, these resources serve as invaluable companions for a seamless and enriching visit to Salem.

Salem invites visitors to embark on a journey of discovery, offering a tapestry of experiences that celebrate its past, present, and future. By immersing oneself in Salem's history, culture, cuisine, and additional resources, travelers can uncover the essence of this enchanting city and create lasting memories of their time spent exploring its streets, landmarks, and hidden treasures.

Printed in Great Britain
by Amazon

48631277R00036